PREDICTING
VOLCANIC ERUPTIONS

PREDICTING VOLCANIC ERUPTIONS

GREGORY VOGT

Franklin Watts ▪ 1989
New York ▪ *London* ▪ *Toronto* ▪ *Sydney*

Library of Congress Cataloging-in-Publication Data

Vogt, Gregory.
Predicting volcanic eruptions / by Gregory Vogt.
p.   cm.
Bibliography: p.
Includes index.
Summary: Describes the technology involved
in predicting volcanic eruptions.
ISBN 0-531-10786-8
1. Volcanic activity prediction.   I. Title.
QE527.5.V64   1989
551.2′1—dc20   89-8990   CIP   AC

*This book is dedicated with
friendship and respect to
George O. Weida,
who is proof that a mind
that never ceases to question,
to learn, and to stand back in
awe at the wonders of life is
a mind that never grows old.*

CONTENTS

PREDICTING
VOLCANIC ERUPTIONS

PREDICTING

ONE

INTRODUCTION: MOUNT PELEE AND MOUNT SAINT HELENS

The signs were all there—sulfurous odors, steam puffs, heavy ash falls, restless and fleeing animals, distant booming sounds, dimming of the sun at mid-day, earth tremors, and changes in the weather—but they were disregarded. At 7:52 A.M. on May 8, 1902, a volcanic eruption killed nearly the entire population of the town of St. Pierre on the Caribbean island of Martinique. Mt. Pelée, a 4,500-foot-high (1,370 m) mountain barely 4 miles (6.5 km) from the town erupted in a rapid succession of three or four violent explosions that kicked up huge dark clouds of super-heated, red-glowing dust. One cloud billowed upward more than 13,000 feet (4,000 m), blacking out the sky as it also spread laterally toward St. Pierre at a speed of perhaps 100 miles (160 km) per hour. In a mere two

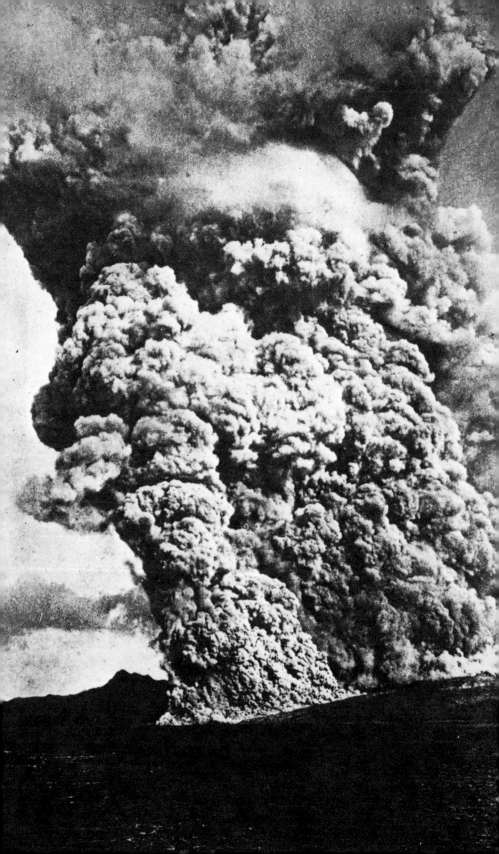

minutes the cloud struck the town and wreaked destruction. Thick-walled buildings were instantly razed by the searing hot dust. Shattered piles of building timbers and trees ignited into huge bonfires. On the docks and in warehouses thousands of barrels of rum, a major export of the sugar-cane-growing region surrounding the town, ignited and exploded sending rivers of flame along the streets. The town became an inferno.

In minutes virtually the entire population of St. Pierre, nearly 30,000 people, perished. People lucky enough to be on the flanks of the hills outside the path of the deadly cloud were stunned as they witnessed St. Pierre disappear in the blackness, only to reappear in the cloud as a vague red glow caused by the blazing fires within.

Days later, only two survivors had been located. One was a young shoemaker named Léon Compère-Léandre. He was on the edge of the cloud and sought refuge inside his house. His skin began to burn as he raced inside the door. The heat was incredible even inside the house. Several others with him in the house died. Later, the young man escaped the heat and ran with bleeding and burned legs for several miles to a nearby town for help.

A second survivor was found within the town itself. August Ciparis, a criminal, had been held in a

The eruption of Mt. Pelée
on the Caribbean island
of Martinique in 1902
killed nearly the entire
population of one village.

low-lying dungeon in the St. Pierre prison. His cell had only a small opening above the door, but it was large enough for a blast of hot air and ash to flash through and sear and burn the hapless criminal's skin. Four days later, rescuers released Ciparis to a world of desolation above. Eventually Ciparis recovered, was pardoned for his crimes, and later, traveled for years with the Barnum and Bailey Circus telling his story and exhibiting his scars.

Seventy-eight years later and 4,600 miles (7,500 km) to the northwest, a mountain in the United States, Mt. St. Helens, also blew up. This mountain, located in the wild and beautiful Cascade mountain range in the state of Washington, was noted for its thick forests, abundant wildlife, and a symmetrical, snow-capped cone rising 10,000 feet (3,000 m) above sea level. The beauty of the mountain and the surrounding countryside made Mt. St. Helens a popular recreation area.

The story of the eruption of Mt. St. Helens was much the same as that of Mt. Pelée, though the death toll was very different. The volcano had lain dormant for more than 120 years. That changed with the start of a string of earth tremors on March 20, 1980. The tremors were detected by *seismographs* in regional scientific laboratories. Seismographs are recording instruments that feel vibrations within the crust of the earth caused by earthquakes and measure their intensity and duration. With three widely spaced seismographs working in concert, measurements can be compared to precisely determine the *focus* of the vibrations. The focus of the March 20 earthquakes was beneath Mt. St. Helens.

Earthquake activity continued, and four days later increased in number and grew into earthquake swarms (combinations of many small and moderately strong earthquakes per hour). The intensity of the quakes was increasing, and this indicated a buildup of pressure within the mountain. On March 27, the first unmistakable sign that the mountain was becoming volcanically active again, a thunderous explosion was heard from the direction of the mountain. A column of steam and ash rose 7,000 feet (2,130 m) from the mountain's summit. A local television news crew, aboard an airplane, circled the mountain. According to reporter Bill Stewart, "There was a hole in the snow on the north side of the peak. It was smudged with black ash, and the top, especially the north side, was shattered." The deep snow at the mountain summit revealed cracks and fissures.

Over the next several days, during occasional gaps in the clouds, geologists who had flocked to the area reported first seeing steam venting and that the hole in the snow had widened. Later, a second hole appeared, and the two eventually combined to make a large, blackened, circular snow crater. Steam, peppered with dust, ash, and coarse particles, began spewing out, darkening the region. The steam continued for nearly a month and then suddenly stopped.

By April 7, the geologists on site noted a bulging of the mountain top almost as though a balloon inside were expanding, pushing the overlying crusty rock outward. Seismographs continued recording earthquakes but detected a decrease in their numbers accompanied by an increase in intensity for the quakes that did occur. Steam venting returned. By now the geologists monitoring the mountain in hopes of detecting patterns in its activity were convinced that something momentous was imminent.

At about 8:32 A.M. on the morning of May 18,

seismometers (instruments that detect earthquakes and send data for seismographs to record) placed in the area of Mt. St. Helens responded to the vibrations coming from a powerful earthquake that struck beneath the volcano. Within 15 seconds the earthquake's shock waves shattered the summit rock and triggered a collapse of the mountain's north flank, resulting in a massive avalanche of rock and ice sliding down the mountain. A few seconds later, Mt. St. Helens blew its top. In a manner similar to the way the removal of a soda pop cap permits dissolved gas in the beverage inside to flash or fizz into bubbles, the rapid removal of rock and ice off the mountain top upset the balance between the pressure produced by the weight of the overlaying rock and the internal pressure of the mountain. Heated water within the molten rock flashed into steam, exploding the side of the mountain outward into a giant "cloud" of shattered rock and dust. In a split second, another explosion followed, but its force traveled upward. A black cloud climbed toward the sky at a speed of 100 miles (160 km) per hour to an altitude of over 60,000 feet (18,300 m).

The enormous lateral blast continued spreading out in a fan shape to a 140-degree-angle. It splintered and knocked down timber in a 232-square-mile (600 square km) area as it swept through the surrounding countryside. The dark tumbling cloud was choked with ash, steam, and hot gases. Its internal temperature was as high as 500° F (260° C), igniting the trees and charring flesh of unlucky animals and humans caught in its path.

Beneath the ash cloud the landslide of rock and ice continued. The eruption's heat began melting the ice, and the resulting water mixed with soil and pulverized rock to create large mudflows cascading down the mountain. More than 0.7 cubic miles (2.9 cubic km) of debris roared downslope and dumped into the North Fork Toutle River valley to the northwest of the summit. Water temperature rose 30 degrees and as many as 70 million fish died. To the northeast, debris also smashed into Spirit Lake. The impact sloshed the lake water out, and when it sloshed back in, the lake bottom was about 295 feet (90 m) shallower than it had been moments before, and the lake's surface was 200 feet (61 m) higher. Now the surface of the beautiful lake was clogged with broken trees and steaming ooze. Somewhere at the bottom was one of the human victims of the eruption. Harry Truman, the 84-year-old proprietor of the Mount St. Helens Lodge on the lake shore, had earlier steadfastly refused even up to the day before the eruption, to evacuate his home to a safer location. Truman's body and bodies of his 18 pet cats would never be found.

In the days following the 1980 eruption of Mt. St. Helens, the magnitude of the destruction became clear. The beautiful cone-shaped mountain now looked, as someone pointed out, like a giant tooth with a cavity. The cavity or crater was 1.2 miles wide and 2.4 miles long (1.9 by 3.8 km). Though most of the debris settled near the mountain base, large regions of the Pacific Northwest was blanketed with ash, in some places as much as 3 inches (7.5 cm) deep. In Yakima, Washington, 85 miles (40 km) to the northeast, it took ten weeks for a city work crew to remove 600,000 tons of ash that the mountain dropped on the city.

The eruptions of Mt. Pelée and Mt. St. Helens both featured devastating lateral blasts. One of the big differences between the two eruptions was the death toll. Mt. Pelée killed as many as 30,000 people while

Steam rises from the floor of
Mt. St. Helens, accompanied by formation of
lava domes. Soon after this photo was taken
on May 30, 1980, a lava eruption occurred.

Mt. St. Helens killed only 60 people. Of course, no major cities were located on the flanks of Mt. St. Helens, but since it was a popular recreation area, many more people could have died. Just prior to the eruption of Mt. Pelée, the people of St. Pierre and the local officials in particular demonstrated an astounding lack of comprehension of what was about to happen to their mountain. The many warning signs were ignored. Instead of evacuating to safety, the people of St. Pierre remained and died. On the other hand, the renewed activity of Mt. St. Helens convinced the scientists on the scene that the mountain was very dangerous. They knew something was about to happen, and upon their advice local authorities restricted access to the areas thought to be potentially most hazardous. Many people heeded the warnings and kept away.

A critical factor determining the death toll of the two eruptions was a greatly improved understanding of the forces at work within volcanoes. Today *volcanologists*, scientists who study volcanoes, travel the world over probing these exceedingly violent, destructive natural forces. They seek to learn much about their nature and consequently the nature of the earth itself. Their work has an immensely practical goal as well—to predict volcanic eruptions. Though the volcanologists who converged on Mt. St. Helens could not say exactly when, they were convinced a major eruption was coming, and their warnings probably saved hundreds of lives.

Today there are more than 600 known active volcanoes on earth. Most of them are located in wide "necklaces of fire" arcing around the boundaries of the slowly moving crustal or *tectonic plates* that carry, like giant rafts, the continents that make up the surface of the solid earth. The majority of these rim the Pacific Ocean basin and are known as the "Pacific Ring of Fire." Indonesia, in the South Pacific, has 100 active volcanoes alone. Many of those have had disastrous eruptions in historic times, such as that of Krakatau in 1883 in which tens of thousands of people were killed.

Another very active volcanic zone is the Cascade Range on the western edge of North America. It falls just east of the margin between the Juan de Fuca and North American plates that are moving next to each other in opposite directions. In this region, more than a dozen volcanoes have erupted in historic time, including Mt. St. Helens in 1980. Also in this region are hundreds of extinct volcanic cinder cones and huge plateaus created by the outflowing of extremely fluid magma (flood basalts).

Hundreds of millions of people live in close proximity to the volcanoes, especially those of the Pacific Ring of Fire. The soil around volcanoes, continuously refreshed by volcanic products, is among the best in the world. Usually in the vicinity is a nearby ocean that serves as a food and transportation source. The economic inducements to live in volcanic areas are therefore strong, and many people choose to live there in spite of the hazards.

For the rest of the world's population volcanoes do not pose an immediate hazard. Volcanoes nonetheless do affect them in ways that can be very significant. On April 5, 1815, the volcanic mountain of Tambora on the distant island of Sumbawa, more than 200 miles (320 km) south of Macassar and 750 miles (1,210 km) east from Batavia, began self-destructing in one of the largest known volcanic eruptions in historic times. The eruption culminated on April 10 and 11 in a series of hellish explosions that disturbed the entire Indonesian island chain.

When the mountain had finished with the worst it had to offer, one third of the rock and soil that made up its original 13,000-foot (3,960 m) height and the lush jungle vegetation that once covered it were gone. In the explosions, thousands of people died, and many tens of thousands perished in the days, weeks, and months that followed from starvation and an outbreak of cholera. However, the human cost of Tambora's eruption was not just limited to Indonesia. The volcano altered the earth's climate for more than a year. Modern geologists, studying the 1815 eruption, have estimated that Tambora blew off with a force equivalent to more than 4,200 hydrogen bombs. It kicked up more than 12 cubic miles of rock (50 cubic km), weighing about 1.7 million tons, into the sky. Much of the debris fell back into the ocean surrounding Sumbawa, but the rest was pulverized so finely that it reached the stratosphere to circle the earth.

After a few months the dust settled out, but the remaining volcanic gas produced a long-term cooling of the atmosphere. In New England, nighttime freezing temperatures persisted into June and well into July. People wore warm coats even during the day. In August, early frosts killed off crops, drastically cutting the harvest. In Europe, the crop loss was hard felt, especially in France where food supplies were already depleted by the Napoleonic Wars. Starving people there were reduced to eating their work animals and even their pets.

PREDICTING

TWO

EARTH DESTROYING, EARTH BUILDING

Volcanoes are at once among the earth's most destructive and most constructive forces. Blasting out millions of tons of pulverized rock to blot out the atmosphere, leaving gaping holes, upwelling lava to flood ravines and valleys, ripping up and engulfing the surrounding countryside in an inferno, and sometimes accompanied by *tsunami* (giant harbor waves) that devastate coastal areas hundreds and even thousands of miles away, volcanoes exact a terrible destruction. Yet the driving force behind eruptions, the upwelling of molten material from the earth's interior, builds up the surface of the earth's crust by spewing fresh rock on the surface and, through its explosions, pulverizing existing rock to later weather into soil.

The roots of volcanoes, within the earth's crust, often contain rich deposits of gold, silver, copper, and diamonds that can be exploited long after the volcanic cone has been weathered away. Under the ocean, a vast network of volcanoes thrusts up to the ocean bottom millions of tons of new crust each day and, at the same time, slowly propels the continents and seafloors in a fluid jigsaw puzzle. In the earth's earliest history, volcanoes boiled out water and gases to add to the world's primitive ocean and atmosphere. Water and gases are still being contributed to the surface by volcanoes today. Volcanoes also blast out millions of tons of glassy dust particles that settle over the earth and break down to release vital plant nutrients such as phosphorous and potassium. Many of the world's richest and most fertile soils have their origins in volcanic devastation.

The planet earth needs volcanoes to renew its surface. The challenge for humans is to learn how to live with volcanoes in relative safety. Understanding what volcanoes are and how they function can lead to forecasting what they might do. An entire branch of the science of geology, called *volcanology*, seeks in part to do just that. Volcanologists seek the answers to many questions: What are volcanoes? Where are they located? Why are they found in the places they are? What is the source of their energy? What are the different kinds of volcanoes and how are they created? Do all volcanoes act in the same way? What happens inside the earth that causes a volcano to erupt? Most important, are there changes taking place inside the earth before a volcano erupts that can be monitored and used as evidence to predict when the eruption will take place?

WHAT ARE VOLCANOES?

A volcano is a hole, called a *vent*, that connects a reservoir of molten rock in the interior of the earth with the surface of the earth. Most magma reservoirs are only 3 to 6 miles deep (5 to 10 km), but molten rock can also form as deep as 60 miles (100 km). Molten rock within the earth is called *magma*, and it travels upward along wide fissures, sometimes under tremendous pressure, to be ejected on the earth's surface. When it reaches the surface, the magma may ooze out and flow like an extremely hot cake batter or become frothy and explode. On the earth's surface, magma is known as *lava*. The lava accumulates and hardens around the vent to form cone-shaped piles or spreads out in wide flows. The cone is also known as a volcano. Many volcanoes have existed for tens of thousands of years and have accumulated, through eruption after eruption, giant cones to become some of the world's loftiest mountains. Mt. St. Helens and Mt. Rainier in the U.S. are volcanic mountains as are Mt. Fujiyama in Japan and Mt. Vesuvius in Italy. The world's tallest mountain, rising over 33,000 feet (10,058 m) from the Pacific Ocean Floor, is Mauna Kea, one of five volcanoes forming the island of Hawaii. It is an active volcano that is still growing.

Through time, people have held some rather strange beliefs as to what volcanoes were. Aristotle, the Greek philosopher, believed volcanoes were to the earth like spasms of disease in the human body. The Frenchman Benoît de Maillet stated, in 1716, that volcanoes resulted from the burning of "oil and fat of animals and fishes concentrated in certain places." According to de Maillet, the animals and

Above: Mt. Fuji, a dormant volcano, is the highest mountain in Japan. Facing: Mt. Rainier, in the Cascade range in Washington State, is a volcanic mountain.

fishes accumulated in sediments following the biblical flood of Noah's time. Antonio-Lazzaro Moro, an Italian of the same period, claimed all the world's land masses were flung out from several titanic volcanoes existing somewhere in the universal sea that covered the earth during its formation.

In Polynesia, islanders believed the goddess Pele, in one of many variations of the story, and her older sister Namakaokahai to be a quarrelsome pair who fought each other in battles ranging over large areas of the Pacific Ocean. Each volcano was the site of one of their battles. Pele was thought to reside in the crater of the volcano Kilauea. When spurned by a handsome Hawaiian chief, she threw an explosive temper tantrum.

In the Mediterranean Sea off Sicily, there is an island that was believed to be the chimney of the forge of Vulcan, the Roman god of fire and the blacksmith to the other gods. As Vulcan beat out thunderbolts for Jupiter, the chief god, hot fragments of lava would erupt up the chimney. The island is known as Vulcano, and from it we derive the world *volcano*.

Science began to enter the volcano picture in the mid-1750s, when geologists began to recognize that in many areas some of the ancient rock resembled the rock recently ejected from volcanoes. Two contrasting schools of geologic thought formed to explain what had happened. One school, the *Neptunists*, believed that all of the land of the earth was formed at the bottom of the ocean from material that precipitated out from the seawater and later was suddenly brought to the surface. The *Vulcanists* forming the other school, believed many of the surface rocks were formed deep within the earth's interior and were suddenly ejected to the surface to build up the land.

The debate lasted for several decades until geologists rejected old ideas that the earth's surface formed suddenly as the result of some great cataclysm. Evidence pointed instead to a slow evolution of the earth's surface and indicated that the remains of earlier ages could be seen in rock. It was also realized that geologic processes taking place today to form new rock and wear away the old must have also taken place in the past. Geologists began to understand the ways rock form and observed that rock building and rock wearing processes often proceed very slowly. When they looked at giant mountains and deep canyons, they realized that such earth features must have taken immense periods of time to be created and that meant the earth itself was very old.

Today volcanoes are recognized for what they are, pressure valves that frequently release heated molten material from deep reservoirs within the earth to its surface. Volcanoes are a major force in the continual evolution of the earth's surface.

HOW VOLCANOES WORK

Through much of the history of the study of volcanoes, the surface effects of eruptions have been at least partially understood. As far back as the A.D. 79 eruption of Mt. Vesuvius, observers have been on the scene taking note of what was happening. In two letters written by Pliny the Younger to the Roman historian Tacitus, there are many objective observations of what took place that are still of use to scientists today for comparison with modern activity of the volcano. What takes place below the surface, however, has not been well understood. Also unknown was why volcanoes existed where they did. Knowing the answers to those questions would lead to the opportunity to forecast new eruptions.

In the early part of this century, an understanding of the subsurface dynamics of individual volcanoes began with the establishment of volcano observatories on Japan (1911) and Hawaii (1912) and the development of seismometers (earthquake sensors) and other measurement devices that could monitor active volcanoes. In the early 1960s further understanding came with the theory of *plate tectonics*. Scientists have long been aware that the continents of the earth look as though they were pieces of a giant jigsaw puzzle. If the pieces were shoved together, they would fit nicely. North America and Europe would merge together and northwestern Africa would slide into the gulf of Mexico, the east side of South America would nestle next to the western side of Africa, and so on. Scientists could see what appeared to be movement of the continents but didn't know how until the theory of plate tectonics was proposed.

The theory of plate tectonics states that the earth's outer solid layer is a huge, slowly changing mosaic of gigantic crustal plates upon which the continents and ocean floors rest. The plates float on an inner layer, which consists of very hot, almost fluid rock. It is something like the way a steel ball-bearing can float on much denser liquid mercury. Each plate moves slowly, at the rate of a few inches per year. As they move, plate boundaries in some places collide while in others they pull apart or slip side-by-side.

The driving force behind the movements of these plates is thought to be thermal convection currents rising from deep within the earth. These currents act much like the movement of boiling water in a pot. Water boils at the pot bottom just above the heating element of the stove. Bubbles rise to the surface and spread out from the middle of the pot to the rim. Water at the rim is a bit cooler than the water at the center, making it more dense and causing it to sink to the bottom. There it moves to the center to be heated and to rise to the surface again. The current is circular. Similar though vastly slower currents are thought to circulate within the earth. Hot earth materials slowly rise in some areas, to be balanced by the subsidence of cooler materials in other areas. When hot materials approach the earth's rocky crust they spread outward, driving the plates above them.

Most volcanoes are found along or near two types of plate boundaries. The first is a *subduction zone*, which is an area where two plates collide, causing one to be driven under the other. The second boundary where volcanoes are often found is a *rift* or a crack where plates are pulling apart from each other.

In subduction zones, the colliding plate boundaries crumple something like the way the hoods of two cars crumple in a head-on collision with one car sliding underneath the other. Most chains of giant mountains are produced by the collision. The thinner, weaker plate is forced underneath the thicker, stronger one. Rock making up the descending plate is ground and heated until it melts and becomes molten magma. Due to the crumpling above, there are many cracks that provide ready vents for the magma to squirt to the surface creating volcanoes (Figure 1).

In rift zones, the plates pull apart from each other leaving deep cracks. Magma from below continuously upwells to fill in the gap forming new crust. Crust that is "eaten" in subduction zones is balanced with the new crust that is formed in the rift zones (Figure 2).

The theory of plate tectonics neatly explains many

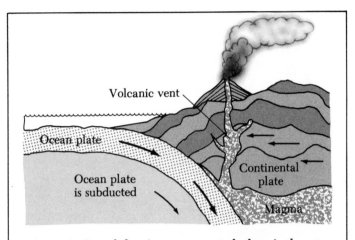

Figure 1. In subduction, one crustal plate is thrust underneath another. Rock is ground and heated and becomes molten matter. The crumpling above creates cracks through which the magma is pushed to the surface.

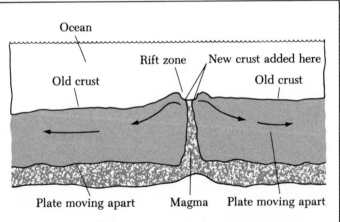

Figure 2. Upwelling magma in rift zones creates new crust.

volcanoes but not all. Some volcanoes, like the volcanoes that compose the Hawaiian Islands, are found in the middle of plates. The island of Hawaii seems to be positioned over a local hot spot or *thermal plume* from the earth's interior. Some geologists have suggested the plume is produced by the heat-generating decay of radioactive isotopes, but no one really knows why it is there. The Hawaiian island chain angles to the northwest in the same direction the tectonic plate it rides upon moves. The oldest and most inactive volcanoes of the chain are at the northwest end, and the youngest and most active volcanoes are at the southeast end. The hot spot remains fixed and creates new volcanoes, forming new islands in the chain while the plate above slides over it.

WHAT HAPPENS
DURING AN ERUPTION?

By traveling the world over, volcanologists have learned there are many different kinds of volcanoes that erupt in many different ways. They visit volcanoes partly because they know their chances of predicting when a volcano will erupt depend, in part, upon understanding what the volcano could do. Knowing that a volcano is likely to create only relatively quiet lava flows means that volcanologists will pay special attention to subtle earth tremors and changes in steam vents and ground temperature in hopes of predicting where the lava will emanate. Volcanologists studying a volcano that is likely to explode will look for those same things but also pay special attention to growing bulges of rock around the cone. The present shape of the volcano plus its eruptive history offers many indications of what it is likely to do in the future.

An individual volcano, however, may behave one way at the beginning of an eruption and another way at the end. This makes predicting more difficult. Furthermore, a relatively young volcano may spew forth liquid lava in long, relatively quiet lava flows, but thousands of years later, when it has aged, the same volcano may clog up, and the resulting pressure buildup will trigger explosive eruptions of such force that it may self-destruct its cone. Knowing eruptive types and what stage the volcano has evolved into is also important.

When a volcano's vent is filled with magma and an eruption is imminent, what happens next is largely determined by three things. The first is the amount of gas present in the magma. Gas-rich magma propels itself to the surface much like the way bubbles expanding in a recently poured glass of soda pop can raise the liquid to overflow the rim. The soda at the bottom is mostly liquid while at the top it is mostly gas. When the bubbles settle on the tabletop, there is a small pool of liquid around the glass. Gas-poor magma, on the other hand, is very sluggish, and will plug the volcano's vent permitting a gradual buildup of pressure to explosive levels.

Another important factor in the eruption is the amount of *silica* in the magma. Silica is a molecule made up of silicon and oxygen. Magmas rich in silica tend to be viscous or thick. Low-silica magmas are generally thin and runny. The difference between high- and low-silica magma is like the difference between hot taffy and warm pancake syrup. In high-silica magmas, gas bubbles have a difficult time escaping, and great pressures build up leading to explosions. In low-silica magmas, gas can bubble to the surface and escape, preventing explosive pressure buildups.

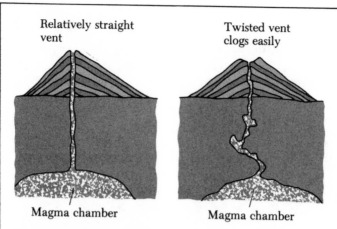

Figure 3. The condition of the volcano's vent affects how it erupts.

The third factor controlling the type of eruption is the condition of the vent (Figure 3). An open vent will allow the magma to flow to the surface in a relatively quiet eruption. A vent closed with debris or hardened lava will cause a tremendous pressure buildup that eventually may shatter the mountain top. Also, the length of the vent that is not filled with lava is important. A vent filled with magma almost to the top of the volcano is most likely to explode laterally and vertically. A vent that is plugged deeply beneath the volcano's summit acts like a cannon. When pressure breaks the plug, gases can shoot up the vent at very high speeds to erupt vertically.

Of course, to have a volcanic eruption it is necessary to have enough heat to melt rock into magma. Just where that heat comes from is not completely understood, but scientists have some good guesses. They know, from laboratory experiments, that rock can melt in one of three ways or a combination of all three. One way to melt rock is to increase its temperature until its melting point has been reached. Another way to cause melting is to reduce the pressure on hot rock. Rock that is hot enough to melt but is under pressure is held in a solid state by the pressure because the pressure raises the melting temperature of the rock. Releasing the pressure permits the rock to melt normally. A third way is the addition of some material that lowers its melting point.

At depths ranging between 60 and 200 miles (97 and 320 km) beneath the surface of the earth, rock is on the verge of melting. The rock might be thought of as existing in a semi-liquid state. Any changes in the environmental conditions there can trigger melting and later a volcanic eruption at the surface.

According to the theory of plate tectonics, surface rock caught in subduction zones (rock being thrust beneath the earth by the movement of plates), will become heated and melt. Often the rock pulled downward is sedimentary rock from the earth's surface. Sedimentary rock has a relatively low melting point. It readily melts when coming in contact with the hot mantle rock. Furthermore, the subducting rock usually carries a small amount of water with it. The water helps to lower the melting point of the rock already there. The magma produced is less dense or more buoyant than the rock below, and it works or floats its way toward the surface in large tear-shaped globs that travel upward along cracks or even melt their way through the material above. Eventually, the magma globs accumulate in the cracks of the crust just a few miles below the earth's surface. The heat of the globs, along with the others that follow it, will melt the surrounding rock, ultimately forming large magma chambers.

The actual eruption of the volcano begins when a pathway to the surface is opened over a magma chamber. An earthquake or even the gravitational pull of the moon may trigger the eruption if the volcano, on its own, is ready to erupt. Pressure over the chamber is suddenly released and the magma flows upward. As we have seen earlier, the content of water and silica and the shape and condition of the volcano's vent will determine the magnitude and kind of eruption. In general, eruption dynamics are very much like popping the cap off a bottle of soda pop. Opening the cap relieves the pressure, and carbon dioxide gas, formerly dissolved in the liquid, bursts into bubbles. If the liquid is saturated with gas, it foams out explosively.

ACTIVE, EXTINCT, DORMANT

Describing the current state of a volcano is sometimes difficult. Some volcanoes may rest thousands of years between eruptions, while others may rest only a few days. Volcanologists use a set of terms that describe volcanoes on the basis of what they are doing at the moment. An *active* volcano is one that has erupted in historic time. An *extinct* volcano is one that is never expected to erupt again. Its last eruption may have taken place so far back in time that the cone has heavily eroded or even disappeared. An active volcano that isn't erupting at the moment is said to be *dormant*. It is expected to erupt again. Often, it is difficult to tell the difference between a dormant volcano and an extinct one because the period of dormancy (time between eruptions) could be longer than all of recorded history. The only descriptive word for a volcano that a volcanologist is 100 percent sure is correct, at the time, is *erupting*.

VOLCANIC ERUPTION TYPES

Volcanoes erupt in many different ways. Knowing the differences between those ways can lead a volcanologist toward a better understanding of what a particular volcano might do in the future. This information can lead to volcano eruption predictions. For example, there is now great concern about future activity of Mt. Vesuvius in Italy. In A.D. 79 Vesuvius erupted in what is now called a Plinian-type eruption, after the Roman author Pliny. The eruption buried the cities of Pompeii and Herculaneum. Volcanologists have learned from studying Vesuvius that it has three different eruption types. Plinian eruptions, which will be described later in more detail, are extremely violent eruptions and occur at Vesuvius at intervals as short as 1,500 years. The last Plinian eruption was 1,900 years ago. A second eruption type mixes explosions with lava flows. These occur about every 100 years. The third type of eruption is much quieter, normally takes place continually, and features minor lava flows and ash release. Concern about Vesuvius comes from the knowledge that it has three eruption types and has been very quiet since 1944. French volcanologist

Crater of Mt. Vesuvius in Italy, site of a famous volcanic eruption in A.D. 79

Haroun Tazieff points out that "minor volcanic activity helps vent eruptive force. . . . When the cork comes out of the bottle, the sudden release of gases accumulated over the last 40 years could lead to a particularly violent eruption." The three different types of Vesuvius eruptions are all due to happen again soon. The longer the mountain is quiet, the greater the probability is that it will erupt.

Some of the major types of volcanic eruptions are described in the following pages. The names are often derived from names of volcanoes. Some volcanologists question the value of such naming, because a volcano can have different kinds of eruptions and peculiar characteristics all its own.

STROMBOLIAN-TYPE ERUPTION

On the Italian island of Stromboli sits a volcano fed with viscous (sticky) magma from below. The magma traps gas and builds up pressure until the volcano "spits" out sticky blobs of lava, called volcanic *spatter* or *bombs*, that shower the side of the cone (Figure 4). At night, the hot fragments can be seen forming luminous arcs through the sky. During active periods, the clots of lava collect on the slopes and stream down the cone in rivulets. Accompanying the shower is a rising white column of steam ("smoke").

Every few minutes or less, a distant "thud" from the volcano, like the thud made when Fourth of July fireworks are launched, is heard by the inhabitants of the island. Suddenly, after decades, an episode may begin in which really large blocks of plastic lava are flung a mile or more from the cone.

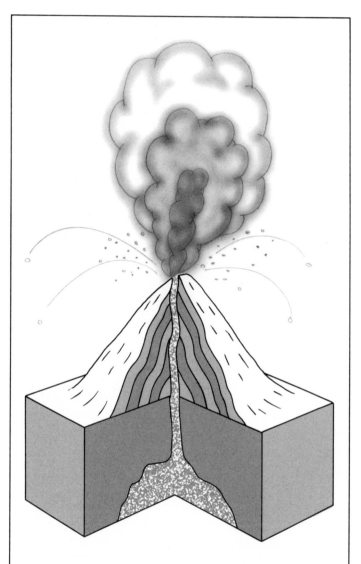

Figure 4. In a Strombolian-type eruption, the volcano spits out sticky blobs of lava because of the high gas content of the magma.

Strombolian eruptions can go on for centuries. One Italian scientist visited the volcano on the island of Stromboli in 1788 and climbed to the summit of the cone to describe this scene:

In the center there was a funnel-shaped tube which contained liquid lava. This incandescent mass was agitated, rising and falling in the tube—the vertical motion a maximum of 20 feet, sometimes slow, other times fast. On reaching a certain height, large bubbles were seen to collect and these bursting with a sharp report carried innumerable fragments in the fiery shower into the air. The lava would then sink in the tube and begin to rise again.

HAWAIIAN-TYPE ERUPTION

Hawaiian-style eruptions are generated from low-silica magma that flows to the surface through the central vent of broadly sloping volcanic cones and through long cracks in the flanks of the cone. Usually earthquakes precede the eruption, forming the cracks through which the lava can pour. Hawaiian magma has a high gas content, but because the silica content is low, the gas can readily escape without dangerous pressure buildups. Near the surface of the vent the gas expands rapidly, causing the lava to spray upward. Along the cracks in the flanks of the cone, stretching a mile or more, "curtains" of lava are sprayed upward.

At the center, lava may accumulate to form a lava lake. The filling may continue until overflowing begins. Fast-moving lava rivers swoop down the mountain and may eventually reach the sea, where their heat explodes the water into steam. The lava may fragment into cinders or harden into pillowlike globs. Elsewhere, the volcano spatters or spills lava that hardens into bubbly sheets of rolling rock or into chunky blocks.

STEAM OR
PHREATIC ERUPTION

Steam explosions sometimes occur when old rock within a volcanic cone is heated by rising magma from below. The heated rock is then contacted by ground water seeping down from above. The contact instantly converts the water to steam, which builds up pressure until the weight of overlying rock can no longer keep it contained. A series of explosions begin that blast out old rock, clogging the vent of the cone and shattering the rock deep within. The shattered rock permits more water to seep in and contact the hot rock. This causes the explosions to continue, possibly for hours. Columns of steam and dust, cinders and ash that can rise several thousand feet into the air come out the top of the volcano.

PLINIAN ERUPTION

The lava that issues from this type of eruption is pastier and stickier than that found in a Strombolian eruption. Between eruptions, the lava forms a thick crust of rock over the crater and plugs the vent. In time, sufficient pressure builds in the magma below to blast out the plug. The force of the explosion may be like a cannon shot that sends debris and gas skyward. A cloud that looks like the trunk of a tall pine tree and then spreads out at the top forms high above the crater in what has been described as a "cauliflower shape." After the clearing of the vent, lava upwells to flow down the volcano's flanks. In some instances, the force of the explosion may be so great as to split the side of the cone so that lava spews forth. One such eruption of Mt. Vesuvius blanketed the city of Pompeii in A.D. 79 with hot volcanic pumice and ash and killed thousands of people. Their bodies were preserved as impressions in the heated ash as it fused together. Today, in archaeological excavations of Pompeii, the impressions have been filled with plaster to reveal the death postures of the hapless victims (Figure 5).

SUBMARINE ERUPTION

Many volcanoes, such as those of the Hawaiian Islands and Iceland, begin their life far below the surface of the ocean. Lava wells up from cracks in the ocean floor to react with the surrounding sea water. Cracks more than about 1,000 feet (305 m) below the ocean surface produce eruptions that are unnoticeable at the water's surface. Water pressure is great enough at that depth to prevent steam from forming. The lava rolls out in pillowlike globs and is called *pillow lava* when hardened. The pillows mount up on both sides of the crack, forming sloped surfaces. The buildup of the pillows carries the top of the vent closer and closer to the water's surface.

At depths shallower than 1,000 feet (305 m), the sea water contacting the lava flashes to steam and bubbles to the surface. Blackish clouds of steam filled with ash and cinders rise up. The ash and cinders

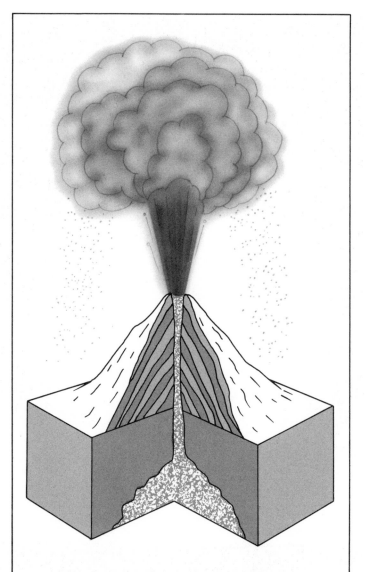

Figure 5. Lava expelled in a Plinian-type eruption is pastier than that in a Strombolian eruption.

eventually accumulate in mounds poking out from the ocean's surface to form small islands. Bubbly pumice rises to the surface to float away in large rafts.

If a submarine volcano remains active long enough, the vent will reach the surface, and the eruption will change character dramatically. Molten lava begins to issue out in large, spattering globs to form a tough cone that covers over and strengthens the ash. If the eruption ceases before the vent emerges, sea waves, in time, will wash away the piles of ash and cinders that make up the island, and no signs of the volcano's presence will be visible on the surface.

PELÉAN OR NUÉE ARDENTE ERUPTION

This type of eruption begins when a viscous, gas-rich magma blows out of a crater. A large volume of gas is produced along with a large quantity of glowing dust, ash, and lava fragments. The eruption may shoot upward with the densest debris falling back to the top flanks of the cone. The debris flows down the side of the cone in a glowing avalanche (in French, called a *nuée ardente*). Pulled by gravity, the avalanche will reach speeds of up to 100 miles (161 km) per hour to obliterate anything in its path. This is what happened with the Mt. Pelée eruption in 1902.

Instead of shooting upward, the eruption may also blast horizontally, as Mt. St. Helens did in 1980.

Eruption of Mauna Loa in Hawaii

Avalanches from horizontal eruptions may begin with an initial speed of up to 300 miles (483 km) per hour.

LAVA FLOODS AND ASH FLOW ERUPTIONS

The most violent volcanic eruptions pale when compared with lava floods and ash flows. Large continental movements and giant earthquakes can rend the earth's crust with "swarms" of fissures stretching hundreds of miles. Lava floods up through the cracks, which may each be 15 miles (24.2 km) long by 50 feet (15.2 m) wide, to cover large plains. Approximately 5 cubic miles (21 cubic km) of lava can flow out from the cracks every day. After a thousand years of eruptions, a 300,000-square-mile (778,000 square km) lava plateau one mile (1.61 km) thick is created. The Columbia River plateau in the Pacific Northwest has been

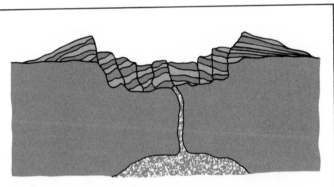

Figure 6. A caldera may form after a volcanic eruption. The overlying volcano collapses into a shallow magma chamber, leaving a wide basin on the surface.

flooded repeatedly by 100-foot-deep (31 m) lava pools as recently as 6 million years ago.

Ash flows form when the ground above large shallow magma chambers is weak. Ash is ejected through long concentric cracks that reach from the surface into the chamber. Large quantities of ash and pumice are produced that flow outward in ground-hugging clouds. The surrounding countryside is inundated. Two million years ago, a 70-square-mile (181 square km) region of New Zealand was buried in such a flow. Entire mountains were covered up in the process. Following an ash flow, the weight of the ground surface above the chamber may be too great for the rock to support itself. The rock may collapse to fill in the emptied magma chamber to form a wide basin called a *caldera* (Figure 6).

PREDICTING

THREE

VOLCANIC LANDFORMS

All of the earth's surface originally came from molten magma. Early in its formation, the earth was a giant sphere of molten rock that slowly cooled to form a hard crust. Wind, water, ice, gravity, and much later, plants altered the volcanic rock that was the earth's initial surface. Surface material was weathered and eroded to be deposited in the oceans to form new sedimentary rock. Today, most of the earth's land surface is covered with sedimentary rock, and none of the original volcanic rock remains exposed. What volcanic material there is on the surface is of relatively recent origin, often in the range of a few tens of millions of years old or less. Volcanic rock form some of the earth's most dramatic, majestic, and fearsome landscapes. The shape of the volcanic landscape is determined by the kind of eruptions that produced them. Runny, low-silica lavas produce gentle slopes. Thick, silica-rich lavas and cinders produce steeper slopes.

Volcanologists study the shape of active volcanoes because it can tell them what kinds of eruptions the volcano experienced previously. This information aids them in trying to predict what is likely to happen in the future.

SHIELD VOLCANOES

Shield volcanoes comprise some of the largest mountains in the world. Volcanoes of this category are built up from thin, free-flowing low-silica lava. When the lava reaches the surface of the vent, it spreads out in circular and fan-shaped flows that eventually build up very broad, gently sloped mountains rarely exceeding a slope of more than 10 degrees. The summits of shield volcanoes contain wide craters that sometimes can fill up with lava during eruptions to form seething lava lakes. In later stages of the eruption, pressure from the weight of the lava lake and the magma below may send lava gushing out from long cracks or fissures radiating outward along the mountain's flanks. The eruption is usually relatively quiet as far as volcanoes go. Although crater walls may crack like a bursting dam to release a river of lava, shield volcanoes rarely explosively self-destruct as some other volcanic types do. Nevertheless, pressures built up from gases within the magma chamber below can shoot up fountains of molten lava more than a thousand feet into the air. Hawaiian-type shield volcanoes are dangerous mainly because the fast-flowing lava rivers released threaten homes and farm lands located on the volcano flanks (Figure 7).

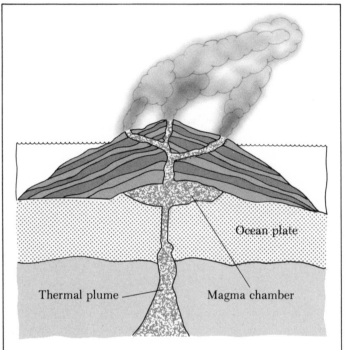

Figure 7. A Hawaiian-type shield volcano is built up from thin, free-flowing, low-silica magma.

COMPOSITE VOLCANO

Composite volcanoes are what most people think of when the word *volcano* is mentioned. They have cones that are much steeper than shield volcanoes, and their bases are not as wide. Their steep, symmetrical cones make them some of the most beautiful mountains in the world. Mt. Fujiyama in Japan is a volcano of this type, as are Mt. Vesuvius and Mt. St. Helens. (In fact, before its 1980 eruption, Mt. St. Helens was known as the "Fujiyama of America" because of its beautiful symmetrical shape that resem-

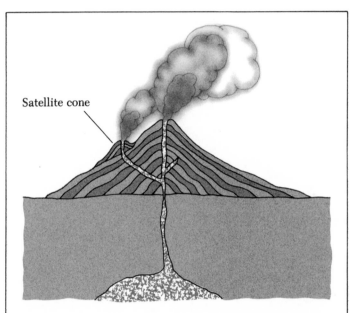

Satellite cone

Figure 8. A composite or stratovolcano is built up from alternating layers of ash and lava eruptions.

bled the famous volcano in Japan.) Composite volcanoes, also called *stratovolcanoes*, are built up of alternating eruptions of lava, volcanic ash, cinders, blocks, and bombs. Lava eruptions produce rivers of lava that cascade down the cone to fan out at its base. These are followed by ash eruptions that build up steep cones. These, in turn, are covered and hardened by more lava flows, and so on. The result is a steep-walled symmetrical cone (Figure 8).

CINDER CONE

Cinder cones are the simplest kind of volcano. A single vent ejects blobs of lava into the air. The gas-rich lava explodes into millions of tiny, frothy globs of lava that harden while still in the air to form cinders. The cinders accumulate into a cone-shaped pile surrounding the vent. If strong winds are blowing from one direction, the cinder cone takes on a stream-lined shape and builds up more cone on the downwind side of the vent. Cinder cones rarely grow more than 1,000 feet (300 m) high.

SATELLITE CONE

Satellite cones are smaller volcanic cones erupting on the side of larger volcanoes. The main shield or composite cone volcano is created, then a fissure opens on its flanks to release lava and ash. The fissure becomes a vent for building up one or more secondary or satellite cones.

CALDERAS

Calderas are not really volcanic cones. They are rather the collapsed remains of volcanic summits following explosive eruptions. What is left is a wide, steep-walled basin several miles across. Crater Lake in Oregon is the caldera left after the ancient Mt. Mazama exploded or fell into itself about 6,600 years ago. Poking out of its center and above the lake level is a cinder cone called Wizard Island.

LAVA DOME

The vents of composite cones often clog with viscous lava. If the magma continues to push up from beneath and does so slowly, the top surface of the clog will cool and harden. The continued pressure forces the hard-ened top to expand, and in doing so it fractures. Lava

Crater Lake in Oregon,
a water-filled caldera

rock tumbles down the side of the clog, which has now taken on a dome shape. As long as the pressure continues from below, the dome will expand. The expansion is slow, like watching the hour hand of a clock, but day after day marked changes in its size become visible. Some lava domes grow hundreds of feet high and may signal the start of a major eruption. The terrible 1902 eruption of Mt. Pelée followed the growth of such a dome, as did the eruption of Mt. St. Helens in 1980.

VOLCANIC NECK

Like the stone columns standing as quiet sentinels on the sites of the ancient buildings of Greece, volcanic necks mark the sites where composite volcanoes once stood. When a volcano becomes extinct, its vent may still be filled with magma. The magma cools and turns into very hard rock. In the process, vertical cracks may develop in the hardened rock and link together to resemble a honeycomb shape when seen from above. Such a feature is called *columnar basalt*. (The same kinds of cracks can also form in thick lava and ash flows when they cool.) Many thousands of years later, erosion wears away the softer rock of the cone to leave tough rock of the vent standing as a high circular tower of rock. The tower is called a volcanic neck. In the movie *Close Encounters of the Third Kind*, the aliens, who come to Earth, land their space ship at a volcanic neck in Wyoming called Devil's Tower.

FUMAROLES, GEYSERS, AND HOT SPRINGS

Hot springs, geysers, and fumaroles are usually found in areas of young volcanic activity (Figure 9). Ground

*Devil's Tower in Wyoming:
a volcanic neck formed by the
erosion of the soft rock of
a volcano cone, leaving behind
the hard interior rock.*

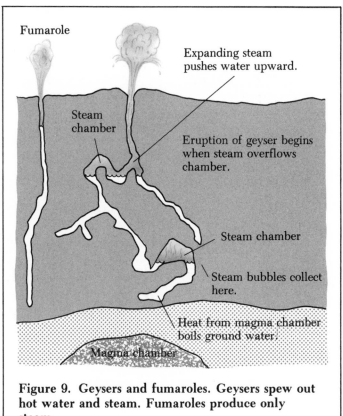

Figure 9. Geysers and fumaroles. Geysers spew out
hot water and steam. Fumaroles produce only
steam.

water seeps downward through cracks to be heated by
the hot rocks surrounding a liquid magma chamber or
surrounding a magma chamber that has recently
hardened but is still hot. The cracks can be thought of
as the earth's "plumbing." If the cracks are relatively
straight with few obstructions, the water will return to
the surface to form bubbling pools of mineral-rich hot

water called *hot springs*. If the plumbing is complicated, with many traps where steam bubbles can be caught for a time, pressure builds up, and suddenly the steam bubbles escape the traps and begin a rush to the surface. Pressure is reduced so rapidly that many more steam bubbles form in the hot water, increasing the rush for the surface. Gushing hot water blows from the ground as *geysers*. As soon as the pressure is released, the gushing stops, and the water seeps back down through cracks to be heated and blown out again.

The Old Faithful Geyser at Yellowstone National Park erupts with hot water every 65 minutes on the average. Other geysers may take days to accumulate enough pressure to erupt. If only steam returns to the surface through the cracks and openings, these holes are called *fumaroles*. Often the steam is laced with chemicals such as hydrogen sulfide (rotten egg gaslike smell), which quickly changes to sulfuric acid and native sulfur that piles in small cones. The acids that accompany fumaroles produce many chemical changes in the surrounding countryside, resulting in dead vegetation and brightly colored rocks.

VOLCANIC PRODUCTS

No other geologic process on earth produces as great a variety of weird and wonderful shapes as volcanoes. The raw material of these shapes is molten magma from deep beneath the earth's surface. Magma usually contains some crystals and fragments of surrounding broken rock. It also contains dissolved gases such as water, hydrogen sulfide, carbon monoxide, and sulfur dioxide. Except for water, all are poisonous gases, and some have a foul odor when released.

*Old Faithful Geyser in
Yellowstone National Park, Wyoming.*

On the surface, lava flows may form a crusty though still flexible surface that twists and rolls as it moves. When cool, the rock surface looks a bit like a pile of rope. This kind of lava is given the Hawaiian name *pahoehoe* (pa-hoy-hoy). If the lava is very crusty and pasty and fractures as it flows, it takes on a blockylike appearance and is called *aa* (ah-ah) in Hawaiian. With many eruptions, globs of lava may be so filled with gas bubbles that the lava takes on a frothy appearance. When it cools, trapped gas bubbles in the rock may make it so light and frothy that it can float on water. Such rock is called *pumice*.

Most lava rock is very dense. If the rock has a low silica content, it cools to become very black. This is known as *basalt lava*. If the lava has a high silica content, it may cool to be rusty red in color. This kind of lava is known as *rhyolite*.

Still other rock types are produced by volcanoes. Material thrown from a volcano may form into plastic, lava globs that are streamlined during their flight through the air and squash on hitting the ground before hardening . These globs are known as *bombs*. Chunks of already hardened lava broken off from a cone are called *blocks*. Some globs of lava cool so rapidly that they become "frozen" in air and have a very glassy appearance. The rock is named obsidian, and small pieces of it may be tear-shaped. Rock collectors call them "Apache tears." Lava fountains may blow out lava in such a way that, when it cools, it resembles hairlike strands of spun glass. This strange product is called "Pele's hair." Rock may also form from the great layers of cinder and ash ejected from volcanoes. When the layers harden, the rock produced is known as *tuff*.

Top: Fresh pahoehoe lava flows in Hawaii.
Bottom: Pumice stones floating in water.

CREATING A
VOLCANO "PICTURE"

As we will see in more detail later, knowing the whole picture of an individual volcano is important for predicting what it might do in the future. Looking at the chemical content of the hardened lava from previous eruptions will indicate if those eruptions were relatively quiet or very explosive. Lava will also indicate trends. If many ancient eruptions were relatively quiet but have since been followed by a newer series of explosive eruptions, future eruptions will probably also be explosive. The shape of the cone will also indicate the relative violence of past eruptions. Its size and the age of its lava and other products will provide an idea of how long the volcano has been around. How eroded the volcano's cone is will provide some indication of how recently the last eruption took place. Each new eruption replenishes a volcano's surface with new lava and other products like ash. The forces of erosion immediately begin to work on the new surface, and the more time between eruptions, the more that can be worn away. A heavily eroded cone could mean the volcano has not erupted for a very long time, therefore is no longer active and not much of a threat to people and property. Volcanologists pull together these kinds of observations and many more to give them a picture they can interpret and use to make forecasts of future eruptive activities.

PREDICTING

FOUR

THE ART OF PUTTING IT ALL TOGETHER

Each year, tens of millions of people are added to the world's population. This means the demand for food and other resources is greater than the year before, and there is a greater need for space where people can live. By necessity or choice more and more people find themselves living near active volcanoes. Increased development near volcanoes magnifies the death and destruction accompanying a major eruption. More than ever before, it has become important to be able to know what volcanoes are up to and to forecast what they will do. An accurate forecast of when a major eruption of a volcano near an urban area will take place could save thousands if not millions of lives by permitting a timely evacuation to a safe distance.

Predicting is the work of volcanologists. As geologists, they also have to be well versed in physics and chemistry. As they study volcanoes, they look at what volcanoes produce (geology), use a variety of instruments to study energy flow beneath the surface (physics), and analyze the composition of the products produced (chemistry).

When a volcanologist makes an eruption prediction, the prediction is an estimate of what will take place. Some volcanologists do not like to use the word *predict* because it sounds too definite. A wrong prediction can lead to public mistrust, much like the moral of the old folk tale about the little boy who cried wolf. When the eruption actually comes, distrustful people may remain in the vicinity until it is too late. Other volcanologists think of predictions as a relatively precise statement of when, where, and how big an eruption will be. Predictions are short-term statements like ". . . in the next 24 hours . . ." or ". . . in the next several days . . ." a dome-building eruption will begin. Forecasts, therefore, are a more general statement like "Mt. St. Helens will erupt again sometime before the end of this century."

Volcanologists, like weather forecasters, work in probabilities. A weather forecaster may say that today there is a 70 percent chance of rain. What this forecast means is that out of 10 days in which the weather conditions are exactly like they are at that moment, it will rain on 7 of those days and not rain on the 3 others. People have become used to weather forecasts such as this and know it is wise to carry an umbrella if the forecast says a 70 percent chance of rain. Working with probabilities, weather forecasters tend to be reasonably accurate in their forecasts over a day or two and less accurate with longer-term forecasts. Still, forecasts can go wrong, and the only way a forecaster can be 100 percent certain of a forecast is to go out and stand in the rain. Then it can be said there is a 100 percent chance of rain at that moment.

Volcano forecasting and prediction, as science, are much less developed at present than weather forecasting. Part of the reason is that every part of the earth has weather at every moment, and there is plenty of opportunity to study weather. However, only few places have volcanic eruptions going on at any one time, and therefore there is less opportunity to perfect the art of volcano forecasting. Forecasting and predicting volcanic eruptions also differ from forecasting the weather in that meteorologists can directly sample weather with instruments on the ground, suspended from balloons and in airplanes, and take measurements with satellites in space. Although volcanologists also take advantage of airplanes and satellites, much volcano forecasting and predicting is based on what is taking place deep beneath the surface of the earth, where it is very difficult if not impossible to send instruments. Volcanologists rather have to rely on surface instruments that infer what is taking place below. Still another reason is that each volcano is different, and each requires individual attention to learn its peculiarities.

In spite of the difficulty of taking the "earth's pulse," volcano-eruption forecasting and predicting are improving in accuracy, and volcanologists look forward to the day when the public will understand and respect their forecasts and predictions the way they respect weather forecasts. Reaching that point will take a great deal of research, but major strides have been made. New scientific instruments and long-term studies are beginning to pay off.

VOLCANO-MONITORING INSTRUMENTS

Volcanologists study volcanoes with the diligence for detail of a Sherlock Holmes. Eruptions and volcanic cones are things they can see and measure directly, but it is equally important to measure things they cannot see. The most important measurements are of the deformation, or change in size and shape, of a volcano's cone and the amount of ground-shaking caused by earthquakes. Growth of a volcano and earthquake activity are the strongest indicators that an eruption is coming. Other forms of measurements, such as gas release from fumaroles and temperature changes, are also important because they help volcanologists to confirm that something is or is not about to happen.

An arsenal of instruments, some simple and others very sophisticated, assist volcanologists in their monitoring of volcanoes.

Seismometers

A seismometer is a kind of "listening" instrument that feels the shakings and tremors caused by earthquakes and movements of magma below the surface. Though the earth is made mostly of solid rock, vibration waves, like waves created on a pond when a stone is tossed in, will travel outward through solid rock when a disturbance in the rock is created. The disturbance is often the snapping movement of two large masses of rock that move in opposite directions along a fault during an earthquake. The movement can trigger a volcanic eruption, as happened with the Mt. St. Helens eruption in 1980. A massive landslide will also send waves through the rock, but even minor disturbances, such as a truck or car passing over a roadway or even footsteps, will also create seismic vibrations.

Seismometers "feel" the earth for its vibrations. They are able to do this because of the property of inertia. Inertia is something that every object has, and it causes objects to resist changes in motion. You can easily experience inertia by tying a cord around a heavy object, such as a book, and suspending the book just above the floor with the other end of the cord held at eye level by your hand. When the book is not swinging, take a quick step. You will observe the book resists the movement and tries to remain where it was. As a result, the book lags behind and begins swinging. Seismometers have small weights suspended inside that also respond to movement in the same way. If the ground upon which the seismometer is placed moves, even so slightly that you are not even aware of it yourself, the weight inside will appear to wiggle. Remember, it is not really the weight wiggling but the ground underneath it doing the wiggling.

The tiny movements of the weight inside the seismometer are picked up by sensors that magnify the movement and send the data to a recording device in a laboratory. The recording device is called a *seismograph*. Seismographs come in many varieties, including needle devices that make zigzag marks on a rotating drum and others that use magnetic tape that can quickly be analyzed by computer (Figure 10).

To be of greatest use, the seismic record has to be compared with information on how far the quake is from the seismograph. This will tell seismologists if the quake is strong or weak. A weak earthquake originating close to the seismometer will register strongly, but a strong quake very far from the seismometer will measure weakly. Consequently, know-

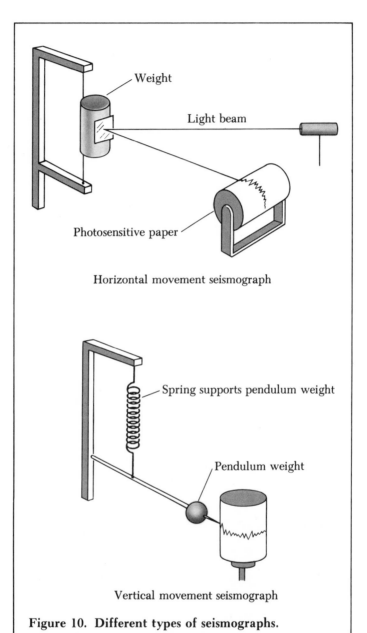

Figure 10. Different types of seismographs.

ing the distance to the source of the earthquake (called the *focus*) is important. The distance is determined by analyzing the record made by the seismograph. Earthquakes put out different kinds of vibrations that travel at different speeds. The seismic record indicates the exact time when each vibration arrives. Working backward from their arrival times and knowing their relative speeds, volcanologists can calculate how far away the focus is. Now, by knowing the distance to the quake and the strength of the vibrations felt by the seismometer, the volcanologist can calculate the real strength of the earthquake.

Earthquakes can sometimes signal the start of volcanic activity. When a volcano explodes, it sends out strong waves through the crust. Prior to that explosion there may be many small earthquakes produced as the uprising magma and steam press on the overlying rock, causing it to expand and crack. There may be several strong quakes per hour or hundreds of small quakes taking place during "earthquake swarms." Both can be signs of impending eruptions.

At the Hawaiian Volcano Observatory on the island of Hawaii, volcanologists are also on the lookout for tremors with their seismometers. These are long-lasting rhythmic vibrations of the rock that may continue for hours. They are caused by movement of magma underground, something like the continuous shaking of the ground caused by a long-rolling freight train. When seismometers detect tremors of sufficient length and intensity, an alarm goes off, indicating to the volcanologists that an eruption may be coming soon.

Also of great importance to volcanologists are the exact locations of earthquakes. Widely spaced seismographs can aid volcanologists in pinpointing these locations. This is possible if the volcanologist has records from three or more seismographs. The distance from each seismograph to the earthquake's focus is first calculated. Then circles are drawn on a map around each seismograph location. The diameters of the circles represent the distance away the earthquake focus is. The earthquake will be found where the three circles intersect.

Earthquake focus location is very useful in determining where a volcano might erupt. If there are many earthquakes in the same location under part of a volcano and if that same location is showing inflation, as measured by tiltmeters and other instruments, it is a good bet that the center of the eruption will be located there.

Tiltmeters

A tiltmeter is an instrument based on a simple idea. When a volcano is nearing an eruption, magma moves toward the surface of the earth. As molten magma moves upward from below, pressure is exerted upward on the solid rock above, causing the volcano to swell or inflate. The swelling can be detected with very sensitive tiltmeters, and the swelling may indicate that an eruption is imminent.

Tiltmeters are like carpenter's levels that contain a small cylinder of liquid with a bubble inside. If the bubble is exactly in the middle of the cylinder, the straight edge of the level is exactly level or horizontal. Volcano tiltmeters are highly sensitive versions of the carpenter's level. They are capable of measuring very tiny swellings of the earth far smaller than the human eye can detect. Some specially designed tiltmeters can even measure the slight movement or tide produced in the earth's rocks from the moon's gravity as it orbits overhead.

One style of volcano tiltmeter uses very sensitive sensors to detect tiny movements in the volcanologists's version of the carpenter's level. Another tiltmeter is a long water-filled tube, its two ends pointing upward, placed at different locations over the volcano. At each end of the tube is a micrometer or very sensitive rulerlike device for measuring tiny changes in water level. If the volcano begins swelling, one end of the tube will rise higher than the other. As this happens, water flows to the lower end of the tube. By measuring its level with the micrometer, volcanologists can determine how much swelling took place in those two locations. You can see how this works by holding the two ends of a water-filled garden hose in your hands. Raise one end and water flows out of the other.

The placement of a tiltmeter on a volcano is important. One end of the meter should point toward the volcano's cone, and the other away. If the near-the-cone end begins rising, the volcano is swelling. If that end lowers, as usually happens after an eruption when the magma chambers deflate, the volcano is shrinking. On the big island of Hawaii, volcanologists have learned that no specific amount of tilt of the Kilauea volcano will tell them when an eruption is about to take place. However, an increase in the rate of swelling tells them that an eruption may be on the way. If the swelling is great or is happening rapidly, the chance of an eruption happening soon is greater. If the swelling is going down, magma may be on the move to erupt in another location. A quiet period may be indicated if no swelling or shrinking is taking place.

Ranging Devices

Volcanologists are interested in the overall shape of the surface of the volcano and of any lava domes that might exist inside its crater. Tiltmeters indicate swelling of a cone because they measure how the volcano's surface beneath them is tilting or rising. However, tiltmeter data alone is insufficient to measure and map the overall shape and size of the volcano. Comparing what the cone looks like now with what it looked like several years, months, or days before can help determine trends of what the volcano is likely to be doing. There could be cause for concern if a lava dome in a crater is getting bigger and the rate of its growth is increasing.

One method for mapping a volcano's shape is to scatter measuring targets that can be spotted from long distances away at key points on the volcano. The targets are anchored to the volcano so that if the targets move, it is really the rock beneath them moving. Using laser ranging devices, the precise distance to the target from a fixed measuring station can be determined. Laser ranging devices calculate the time a laser beam takes to travel to the target and bounce back again. Because we know the speed of light, the distance between the target and the station can be calculated. This distance is then marked on a map along with all other distance measurements to show change in the volcano's size. On the same map the tiltmeter measurements are also plotted. Combining tiltmeter and range measurements provides a complete picture of the volcano's deformation. A slow expansion of the cone could mean an eruption is on the way, though it still may be years off. A rapid expansion may indicate a critical state has been reached in the volcano that will lead to an eruption.

Another device for measuring distances around volcanoes is an extensiometer (Figure 11). Two posts are anchored in the surface of a volcano on the floor of a crater. A wire or a rod is extended between the posts and fixed firmly to one. If the distance between the two posts changes, the length of the wire or rod between them will also change. How much one or both posts have moved can be read directly from the instrument, or it can be electronically measured and transmitted to a monitoring station.

A less technical way of measuring distances is done with a steel tape measure. Very long tape measures are extended between various known points on a periodic basis. If the distances measured are

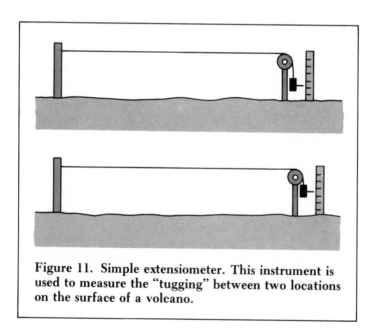

Figure 11. Simple extensiometer. This instrument is used to measure the "tugging" between two locations on the surface of a volcano.

different, volcanologists will know if there has been some inflation or contraction of the volcano. To be accurate with a steel tape, the people holding the opposite ends must extend it with just the right amount of pull so that it is tight but not stretched (making it longer than it really is). A spring device helps them determine just how much to pull. An adjustment even has to be made for temperature changes. Steel tapes lengthen when they heat up, and measuring distances around volcanoes can be a hot business.

Still another method of measuring a volcano's shape is very simple. Photographs of the volcano are taken from different fixed locations over time. If the volcano has changed significantly, comparing old and new pictures will reveal this.

Gas Sniffers

Volcanoes are prodigious producers of gas. They release carbon monoxide, carbon dioxide, hydrogen sulfide, chlorine, and hydrogen chloride, sulfur dioxide, and water vapor as well as other gases. The quantity of gas released from a volcano and its composition varies through time. What is released depends upon many factors including how deep magma is below the surface, whether or not the magma is moving, and the number of cracks in the cap rock above, which permit gas to travel to the surface where it can be measured.

Volcanologists take gas samples by inserting snorkel-like devices into the gas escaping from fumaroles. The gas is sucked into the snorkel and saved for later analysis in a laboratory or sent into a small, transportable, chemical-analysis instrument for an immediate readout of its contents. A glass vacuum tube may also be used for sampling gas. One end of the tube is broken and held in the escaping gas. The tube fills with the gas sample and then is sealed off by melting the end with a torch or just by touching it to some nearby hot lava. The tube is then returned to the lab for analysis. Another method for taking gas samples is to place the sampling equipment on an airplane and fly through the gas plume that is being released by the volcano.

By studying volcanic gas, volcanologists have noted that the quantity of water vapor in the gas often increases before an eruption. Increases in carbon dioxide and sulfur dioxide also seem to precede eruptions. Studies of the Kilauea volcano in Hawaii have shown that the amount of hydrogen gas escaping from a volcano can increase a few days or hours before an eruption. Hydrogen monitors are placed in areas of volcanic gas. The sensor works on the same principle by which many spacecraft with human crews get their electricity in orbit. Such spacecraft power systems will combine hydrogen gas with oxygen in a special device called a fuel cell. When the two gases combine, they produce water and generate electricity. A fuel cell in the hydrogen sensor generates electricity when hydrogen gas enters it and combines with oxygen supplied from a compressed gas cylinder. The more hydrogen gas, the more electricity. The amount of electricity that is produced is transmitted by radio every ten minutes to a laboratory where volcanologists can study the readings and look for changes in hydrogen release.

Other scientific studies are examining the presence of trace elements of gold, platinum, and iridium in venting volcanic gas. Scientists looking for these and other trace elements believe increases in the amount of these elements signal that molten magma is moving into the volcano.

Gas studies of volcanoes are still experimental for the most part. By themselves, increases in various gases do not clearly signal the start of a new eruption, and much more needs to be learned about gas release in order for it to be a reliable eruption indicator.

Infrared Scanners, Pyrometers, and Thermocouples

Volcanologists sometimes do seemingly strange things. During an eruption, when people are fleeing the scene, volcanologists may move toward the eruption site to make scientific observations, including taking the temperature of the lava and sampling its composition. Such an act might seem dangerous, but with caution and fireproof clothes, temperature measurements can be done safely.

Temperature measurements before, during, and after eruptions provide valuable data. A warming trend may indicate a greater chance of eruption. A cooling trend will indicate a trailing-off of an eruption or even a quiet period for the volcano.

Different tools are used for volcano temperature measurement, depending upon what is happening at the moment. Infrared radiation scanners are especially valuable for detecting a warming or cooling trend. Infrared radiation is an invisible form of light given off by heat. Sensing devices can be tuned to look for this radiation. These devices are called *infrared scanners* because they break up the scene they are looking at into points arranged in rows like the lines on a television set. Objects that are warm emit more infrared radiation than objects that are cool and appear as bright areas on the scan. Infrared scanners can be carried by hand, in airplanes for over-flights of a volcano, or on satellites in space. If repeated scans of a volcano show areas that are getting brighter, volcanologists interpret it to mean the volcano is heating up. The heating is usually due to magma moving closer to the surface, and the area of greatest heat intensity could be the spot where magma will actually erupt onto the surface.

An accurate way to measure the temperature of erupting lava is to use an *optical pyrometer*. This device can be used to measure the temperature of fountains of hot lava being ejected from the volcano. Under such conditions, it is dangerous to get too close, and the volcanologist will hold up an instrument through which the glowing lava can be seen. In a second viewing-window of the instrument is an iron wire that is heated by electricity. The wire begins glowing red but will change to white when very hot. The volcanologist adjusts the amount of current running through the wire so that the wire's color matches the color of the lava. At that point the temperature of the wire, assumed to be the same as that of the lava, is measured. White hot lava is 2,190 degrees Fahrenheit (1,200°C), yellow 2,010°F (1,100°C), orange 1,650°F (900°C), bright red 1,290°F (700°C), and dull red 930°F (500°C).

A more accurate temperature measurement of active lava is made with a *thermocouple*. A thermocouple is a pair of twisted wires made of two different metal alloys. The wires, at the end of a ceramic rod, are thrust directly into hot lava. The heat produces a flow of electricity between the two wires that can be measured. The hotter the lava, the more electricity flows. The amount of electricity produced can be measured, and from this the temperature of the lava can be calculated. Sometimes volcanologists will walk out on lava lakes that have hard crusts formed over them. They will drill holes in the hardened lava and thrust the thermocouple into the molten lava below.

Electromagnetic Studies

Volcanologists have noted that changes in temperature and pressure can affect electrical and magnetic properties of rocks. When rock temperature is above $1,110°F$ ($600°C$), it loses its magnetism. Molten basalt is nonmagnetic. Hardened basalt has a slight magnetic field that can be detected. Molten rock is a good conductor of electricity, and hardened rock is not. Periodic magnetic checks of a volcano with a magnetometer will reveal temperature changes inside if the magnetic field has gotten stronger or weaker. A magnetic field that has disappeared could mean that magma is moving upward, and an eruption could take place soon. An increase in the electrical conductivity of a volcano may mean the presence of new magma.

Magnetic measurements are made by taking a magnetometer around the volcano to produce a map of the strength of its magnetic field. A pair of electrodes (electrical contacts) planted in the volcano can be used to measure the electrical resistance of the rock between those two points. The intensity of the change of the rock's electrical resistance will indicate temperature, pressure, water, and even chemical changes taking place within the volcano. All of these changes can be expected when a volcano is getting ready to erupt.

Electromagnetic studies of volcanoes are still highly experimental, and much is yet to be learned about interpreting data gathered by them. Only when supported by many other kinds of better understood observations do electromagnetic studies assist in forecasting. That should change as more research is done in the field.

Gravity Meter

All matter has the attractive force of gravity and pulls on all other matter. The amount of gravity is in part determined by density. The more matter packed in an object, such as a volcano, the greater its density and therefore the greater its gravitational attraction. Volcanologists know that within volcanoes, prior to erupting, large-scale movements of magma take place. The movement of magma changes the amount of matter present. Hot, gas-rich magma is less dense than solid rock, and therefore its presence within a volcano can lower the volcano's gravitational attraction. The amount of that reduction in gravitational force is very slight, but it is possible to measure it with portable gravity meters. Gravity meters can detect a gravity change of only one millionth of one percent.

Gravity surveys of quiet volcanoes are made. The volcanologist will place the gravity meter at many locations on and around the volcano. It is important that the locations chosen are mapped precisely for elevation, because if the elevation is off even by a few inches, the gravity meter will give a false reading indicating a greater or lesser magnetic pull at that location than is really there. At a later date, a second survey is made at the very same locations. A change in gravitational pull may indicate the subsurface movement of magma that might be leading up to a new eruption of the volcano.

Biology

There are many stories of animals acting strangely just before catastrophic events. Animals were reported fleeing the site of Mt. Pelée before it erupted. Like rats leaving a sinking ship, the behavior of animals could indicate something is about to happen. However, as a volcanic predictor, animals are not very reliable. Often they too get caught, just like humans, when a volcano explodes.

Plants, on the other hand, could provide clues to the movement of magma. An area of dying vegetation could indicate new hot ground heated by magma near the surface. Dying vegetation could also indicate a new area of volcanic fumes being released. Patches of dead vegetation are very obvious indicators to volcanologists, flying overhead making aerial surveys, that something is changing.

Historical Studies

Another valuable predictor of volcanic eruptions is historical study of the volcanoes. Volcanologists can scour the surface of a volcanic cone, probe into cracks in the lava, and drill holes in the lava to reconstruct its history for thousands of years. Lava is laid down on a volcanic cone like sheets of paper stacked one at a time. The top sheet was placed there most recently, and the bottom sheet was placed first. By probing deep into the layers of the lava, the volcano's history can be read like a book. With careful dating, the age of each page (lava layer) can be determined so that an eruptive history can be calculated. In other words, if the volcano's cone is built up of 300 layers of lava, produced from 300 different eruptions, and the oldest layer is 30,000 years old, the volcano has erupted once on the average every 100 years. For the future this means that the volcano is likely to erupt again 100 years after its last eruption. This, of course, assumes the volcano will continue the same pattern in the future. If the last eruption was 90 years ago it is a good, but not a sure, bet the volcano will erupt again in the next ten years. Remember, 100 years is just the average. Eruptions of 150, 100, and 50 years average out to 100.

Forecasts based on averages do work fairly well. Two geologists who had studied the eruptive cycle of Mt. St. Helens for many years concluded in 1978 that Mt. St. Helens had been the most active and explosive volcano in the contiguous 48 states over the last 4,500 years. By examining the rocks created by the volcano, they learned that it had a long history of creating viscous lava domes, lava flows, avalanches of hot rock, explosions, and mudflows. Piecing together the ages of various eruptive episodes, the geologists concluded Mt. St. Helens erupted on the average every 225 years. They concluded their study by predicting the volcano would erupt sometime in the next 100 years and probably before the end of the century. Two years later, Mt. St. Helens erupted.

PUTTING IT TOGETHER

The end result of the data gathered from tiltmeters, seismometers, gas samples, electromagnetic and gravity measurements, and historical studies is a scientific "picture" of the volcano. The volcano's past and its current condition are known in very general terms. Volcanologists will stand back and gaze at the picture to interpret its meaning. No one piece of the picture, such as recent earthquake activity or an increase in steam, by itself conclusively points to an eruption.

What counts is how all the different pieces fit together. It wasn't until the last weeks before Mt. St. Helens exploded that the volcanologists had enough data to confirm their suspicions that something big was about to happen. Among their accumulations of data were earthquake swarms, bulging of the volcano's north flank, and periodic steam and cinder outbursts. They gained this information by studying the data provided by seismographs and tiltmeters and through the use of various distance-measuring techniques.

The scientists working on the mountain paid very close attention to the exact locations of earthquakes under the mountain and related them to the locations where the volcanic dome was inflating. Near the time of the eruption, they discovered changes in size averaging about 6½ feet (2 m) per day on the north flank of the cone. In that manner, they were able to conclude that magma was working its way into the area just beneath the north side of the summit. The evidence suggested to the scientists that there was a great danger of a large avalanche and a catastrophic blast. That information led public officials and lumber operations working in the area to restrict access to the mountain. Undoubtedly many lives were saved by keeping tourists and others at a safe distance.

Another story is less well known. In 1983, the Indonesian island of Una Una was shaken with earthquake swarms. Seismographs enabled geologists to fix the location of the earthquakes. They were located within the Colo volcano on the island. A few days later, small explosive eruptions began. Based on its current rumblings, what little was known about the history of the volcano, and the behavior of other volcanoes in the region, Indonesian volcanologists suspected the volcano was very dangerous and recommended the island be evacuated. Public authorities there, very familiar with volcanic eruptions, needed little encouragement, and they quickly agreed that evacuation was a good idea. Soon, all 7,000 inhabitants left the island by boat. A short time following their departure, the Colo volcano climaxed its eruptions by issuing hot pyroclastic flows that swept over the island, killing its vegetation, livestock, coconut plantations, and destroying housing. The devastation was complete, and years will be required to rebuild the island's economy. The important fact of the story is that the island's people are alive to rebuild.

MORE SUCCESSES

Since the May 1980 eruption of Mt. St. Helens, the staff of the Cascades Volcano Observatory has gained enough information about the mountain to predict successfully most of its subsequent dome-building eruptions as much as three weeks in advance. With a network of seismographs and other instruments, the volcanologists have gathered data about earthquake activity and its location and about deformation (changes in its shape) of the crater floor and lava dome, and have sampled the kinds, quantities, and temperature of gas emissions. Their experience on the mountain has shown them that inflation in the crater typically begins a few weeks before an eruption occurs, and the rate of inflation may accelerate when the eruption is close.

A new and intriguing theory about Mt. St. Helens's eruptions has come from comparing dome growth and shallow earthquakes to the cycle of the moon. As the moon orbits the earth, the combined gravitational attractions of the two bodies produces a tide that raises the water in the oceans in some places and lowers it in others. As the earth rotates, the tides follow. This same tidal effect also causes the land to rise slightly. The amount of rising is too slight for people to notice, but scientists speculate it could affect the balance of magma pressure with its overlying rock inside the volcano. In all but 3 of 17 periods of renewed activity of Mt. St. Helens that were studied, most changes took place following the maximum tidal effects produced by the moon and before the tide was at its lowest. If a relationship between land tides and eruptive activity does exist, volcanologists will have another important indicator that could help them predict future eruptions of the mountain.

Scientists working in Hawaii have come to know the Kilauea volcano so well that they have been very successful in making short-term predictions. Scientists in the Hawaiian Volcano Observatory study earthquake records and are able to guide field research teams by radio to within a few hundred meters of the actual site of lava outbreak. When necessary, people in the area are alerted to the start of the new volcanic activity and evacuated to safety in plenty of time. Since 1979, all eruptions have been successfully predicted.

As more and more individual volcanoes are closely monitored, their mechanisms become better understood, and it becomes easier to recognize the signs that changes leading to an eruption are taking place. The major problem facing volcano prediction efforts today is determining not the start of an eruption, but what it will do once it has erupted. Of the 100 or so volcanoes that erupt around the world every year, only one usually develops into a major life-threatening event like the 1902 Mt. Pelée eruption or the 1815 Tambora eruption. Normally there is time to evacuate people to a safe distance. In many cases, it is not necessary to evacuate people at all because the eruptions never escalate to major proportions. The question becomes "Which volcanic eruption will remain relatively mild, and which will destroy mountains or unleash major pyroclastic flows?" Knowing how an eruption will change is one of the major challenges in volcano research today. It is a challenge because many of the signs that are useful in predicting the onslaught of an eruption, such as inflation of the summit and greatly increased earthquake activity, have been relieved by the flow of magma on the surface. During an eruption, the signs become more difficult to read and make sense of. The solution to this problem may, in part, be met by continuous monitoring of volcanoes around the world and by the use of computers to correlate data from many volcanoes to better understand the dynamics of eruptions.

PREDICTING

FIVE

VOLCANOES IN OUR MIDST

Whether you live on the flanks of volcanoes or far from them, volcanoes are a part of your life. A major eruption on the other side of the world could blast dust and gases into the stratosphere to diminish sunlight, altering the whole world's climate for a year or more. You may find yourself wearing warm jackets on summer days. Farmers will experience shorter growing seasons, and produce at the grocery stores will be less abundant and more expensive. In poor countries famine could be triggered, resulting in tens of thousands of deaths due to starvation.

In this century alone, an average of more than 800 people have died each year due to volcanic eruptions. Through 1982, in one estimate, volcanoes have been claimed responsible for more than $10 billion in damage to buildings, roads, and agriculture. The costs of volcanoes affect each of us directly as victims or indirectly as providers of aid to disaster areas.

CONTROL EFFORTS

In spite of the volcanic threat, hundreds of millions of people around the world live on or near volcanoes. When a volcano does erupt, many people flee the danger, but others stay and fight back. Little can be done when a Mt. St. Helens or a Mt. Pelée explodes and blasts forth pyroclastic flows to bowl over and incinerate nearly everything in its path. Actions can be taken, however, when rivers of hot lava threaten villages and homes.

The first recorded attempt to do something about lava flows took place during an eruption of Sicily's Mt. Etna in 1669. In March of that year, the volcano began with a series of earthquakes that culminated in the most violent eruption in the volcano's history. Ash was sprayed over the countryside in great fans stretching out as far as 60 miles (97 km) from the cone. A great flow of *aa* lava (see page 62) surged down the mountain, heading directly for the city of Catania. *Aa* lava flows are sticky and sluggish, cool rapidly on their sides and harden and form natural levees. The hot lava in the middle of the levees continues downslope while adding new levees at the end of the old. The levees form a trough through which the lava flows, preventing it from spreading out.

The tongue of lava stretching down Mt. Etna toward Catania brought out a stalwart citizen named Diego de Pappalardo. Wearing wetted cowskins for protection from the lava's blast-furnace heat, de Pappalardo and three or four dozen fellow citizens climbed the mountain high above their city. Using long iron bars, de Pappalardo and the others poked at the natural levees and succeeded in breaching the walls, releasing the lava. As they hoped it would, the main stream of the lava slowed and a new stream headed to the northwest straight toward the village of Paterno.

The advance of the new lava tongue was greeted with anger by the citizens of Paterno, and at least 500 of them marched, armed with whatever weapons they could find, on de Pappalardo and his people. They succeeded in discouraging the lava-flow control efforts, and soon the breach in the lava channel healed itself, permitting the original flow to Catania. In time the flow reached the city, and the city's old high walls succeeded for several days in diverting the flow around the city to the ocean. Eventually, the pressure from the flow was too great, and the wall broke in a weak place, permitting the lava to flow through the middle of the city, nearly filling up the harbor.

Three hundred years later, another attempt at controlling volcanoes took place. Mauna Loa erupted on the island of Hawaii in November 1935. Huge quantities of lava issued above the surface, which for a time pooled in a large depression between the slopes of Mauna Loa and the quiet Mauna Kea volcano. By December 22, the lava pool that had formed broke forth and sent a 2,000-foot (609 m) lava flow that headed straight for the coastal city of Hilo at a rate of 1 mile (1.6 km) per day.

Thomas Jaggar, the head of the Hawaiian Volcano Observatory at the time, decided to try a daring experiment to divert the flow of the lava. A friend once suggested controlling lava flows with explosives. Jaggar seized on the opportunity to test the idea.

Jaggar's experience with Hawaiian volcanoes taught him that the pahoehoe lava (see page 62) advancing toward Hilo would form hard crusts completely surrounding the flow. Such crusts, up to 2 feet thick (0.6 m), will form *lava tubes* like sewer pipes, through which the hot liquid lava continues to flow. Jaggar reasoned that explosives could be used to disrupt the tunnels and hopefully clog them with chunks of hardened lava or at least divert or somehow change the flow direction.

Jaggar selected the main channel of the flow at an elevation of about 8,500 feet (2,590 m) up Mauna Loa. Twin-engine Keystone bombers of the U.S. Army Air Corps took off with 600-pound (272 kg) TNT bombs and 300-pound (136 kg) black powder bombs. Jaggar later described the assault:

> *The entire operation was spectacular and impressive. Amid the thunder of shattering explosions, masses of rock and sheets of glowing lava were hurled in all directions. Many of the great bombs, dropped from planes traveling at high speed, plunged directly into the open channels through which molten lava was flowing, while others crashed upon the roofs of tunnels, blowing them open and releasing the melt imprisoned within, causing it to gush upwards and commence spreading immediately.*

The results of Jaggar's experiment were mixed, and many volcanologists now consider it a failure. Thirty-three hours after the bombing had begun, the lava flow stopped. The eruption was coming to an end, and the bombing may have had little to do with stopping the lava's advance. Several hours later, the lava resumed its advance and then stopped for good, 12 miles (19 km) outside of town.

In 1955, another control method was employed during the eruption of Kilauea. Gordon Macdonald, the Hawaiian Volcano Observatory's chief scientist, tried a simple but effective experiment. He placed a wooden plank on its side directly in the path of a lava flow. Macdonald braced the plank and angled it to see if it would divert the flow. As he hoped, the lava reached the plank and headed off in a new direction. The diversion technique worked for 30 minutes until the wood of the plank was burned away.

Next, Macdonald supervised a team of six bulldozers that pushed up a dirt wall 1,000 feet (305 m) long and 10 feet (3 m) high in the path of a flow that was heading toward a sugar plantation camp. Again the lava was deflected by the obstruction, but the lava flow ceased only after having traveled 50 feet (15 m) along the barrier. Unfortunately, other lava streams later reached the plantation camp by different routes and wiped it out.

In the North Atlantic island of Heimaey off the coast of Iceland, the Helgafell volcano erupted in January of 1973. A 5,000-foot (1,524 m) fissure opened, and streams of lava gushed forth. A wall of lava 120 feet (37 m) high and 1,000 feet (305 m) wide began moving toward the harbor. All but 300 of the island's inhabitants were evacuated from the island. The remainder stayed behind to fight the lava's advance.

They selected to spray seawater on the advancing lava to cool it and cause it to harden to form its own dam and at least slow its flow. At first, fire engines blasted the front of the flow with water. The lava front hardened and formed small barriers. However, the advance of the lava from behind quickly overwhelmed the barriers.

The Icelanders soon realized that their efforts would be more effective if they were directed further back in the flow. Huge pumps sprayed deluges of seawater at several points in the flow in the hope of cooling the lava enough to create several internal barriers of hardened rock. By early July, the eruption stopped, and so did the lava flow. A total of 43 pumps and more than 19 miles of pipes were used in attempting to stem the flow. While the flow was never stopped, the efforts did seem to slow its advance, and in the end, Heimaey's harbor was saved.

AN AVALANCHE OF DEADLY MUD

On November 13, 1985, the worst volcanic disaster since the 1902 eruption of Mt. Pelée took place. The pilot of a DC-8 cargo jet had a bird's-eye view of the beginning of a catastrophe that was to take many lives. Shortly after 9 P.M., pilot Manuel Cervero was passing 7,000 ft (2,130 m) over the top of the 17,716-foot (5,400 m)-high Nevado del Ruiz volcano in Colombia. When his plane was almost precisely over the top of the volcano, a strong eruption began. "First came a reddish illumination that shot up to about 26,000 feet (7,925 m). . . . Then came a shower of ash that covered us and left me without visibility. The cockpit filled with smoke and heat and the smell of sulfur." Though the nose of the DC-8 was sandblasted as it flew through ash, the pilot managed to land the plane safely. People on the ground, however, did not fare so well.

Nevado del Ruiz volcano in Colombia shortly after its deadly eruption in 1985 that killed over 20,000 people.

Nevado del Ruiz had not had a major eruption since 1845 and seemed safe to many of the inhabitants of the region. Its last major eruption covered the area with some 250 million tons of lime mud that eventually decomposed into a rich topsoil, supporting a prosperous cotton- and rice-growing agriculture. Thirty miles (48 km) from the volcano was the Colombian town of Armero in which more than 22,500 people lived.

The eruption actually began with steam explosions shortly after 3 P.M. Ranchers to the north of the mountain heard a deep rumbling sound and looked to see a black cloud rise from the summit. A fine ash began falling on the town of Armero at about 5 P.M. Townspeople in several communities began smelling a strong sulfurous odor.

At 9:08 P.M. the eruption intensified with two strong explosions that were heard more than 18 miles (30 km) away from the crater. Pyroclastic flows surged from the volcano's crater and spilled outward over the mountain's ice cap in glowing rivers of fiery hot ash and cinders. The heat from the flows melted part of the ice cap, and the resulting water mixed with soil and ash to form massive waves of mud that began rushing down the mountain's flanks. The flows stripped bark from shrubs and swept up trees, rocks, and soil. The debris-choked mudflow merged with the water of the Las Nereidas, Molinos, Guali, Azufrado, and Lagunillas rivers. The Lagunillas River was already engorged from the torrential rains of the past week, and now it was a wall of muddy water that raced down the river valley at speeds of up to 25 miles (40 km) per hour. At the outside of a sweeping curve of the valley lay the city of Armero.

Many of the residents of Armero were in bed when the torrent of mud reached the city. A natural dam was quickly breached by the flow, and the mud entered the town in a wave shortly before midnight. Several more waves of mud followed. Many people were entombed as the mud squashed their homes. Those people outside at the time fared only slightly better. Hortensia Oliveros ran into the street with her 11-month-old daughter and her husband and mother after being awakened by screaming in the streets. Within moments, a wave of mud swept them all off their feet. The force of the mud yanked her daughter out of her grasp, and the mud carried each family member away in different directions. Hortensia, the only family member to survive, was later pulled from the mud by a taxi driver.

Hortensia's story was typical of the hapless survivors. Rescuers found some survivors stuck up to their necks in the mud. Most of the town's residents, however, were buried deeply. A few survivors, saved by the high ground they were standing on, told of how they were horrified as they witnessed a large swath of the town disappear under a wall of mud. One survivor said the mud ". . . rolled into town with a moaning sound like some sort of monster." More than 80 percent of the town's buildings disappeared in a wave of slime.

All told, 5,150 homes were damaged or destroyed in the region. Fifty schools, two small hospitals, and many miles of roads, railroad lines, and electric transmission lines were wiped out. Hundreds of small and large industries were destroyed, and several square miles of prime agricultural land were covered in mud. The human toll was far worse. Approximately 22,000 people died and another 10,000 were injured.

Like so many other disastrous volcanic eruptions of the past, Nevado del Ruiz announced its intentions of erupting. A year before, mountain climbers at the summit noted that fumaroles in the small Arenas Crater on the northeast edge of the mountain's ice cap had increased the amount of gas they released. That same month, earthquakes were felt near the summit of the mountain. The earthquakes and unusually high fumarole activity continued through the next year. Two months before the November 13 eruption, steam eruptions from the volcano lasting several hours ripped out boulder-sized blocks from the throat of the volcano and shot out small showers of rock and ash. The shaking coming from the eruption broke loose an avalanche of debris that severed a valley road many miles away.

Volcanologists, concerned by the persistent earthquakes, fumarole activity, and steam eruptions had warned for nearly a year that Nevado del Ruiz might have a major eruption. Just when the eruption would take place was unknown, but they knew it was coming, for it was the mountain's history to do so. Over the last 10,000 years it had erupted at least ten times, and during each eruption major mudflows were unleashed.

Fear of what Nevado del Ruiz might do led to the establishment of a small network of scientific instruments, including seismographs and tiltmeters, set up around the mountain to get a better picture of where the earthquake activity was centered and whether the volcano was inflating with new hot magma. Between July 20 and October 26 alone, 1,350 earthquakes had been recorded, averaging about 15 per day.

Just over one month prior to the eruption, a report published by the Colombian National Institute of Geological-Mining Investigations warned of the certainty of disaster and even singled out the city of Armero and the village of Chinchiná on the opposite side of the mountain as threatened sites. The report included a geological-hazards map that identified the areas of greatest danger during an eruption and clearly placed the town of Armero in the danger zone. The report predicted that there was a 100 percent probability that potentially damaging mudflows would be unleashed during the eruption. The report further stated the chance of a regional ash fall was 67 percent. Less likely, according to the report, were pyroclastic flows (21 percent), lava flows (8 percent), and a lateral blast from the volcano's cone (7 percent).

Official action on the danger was slow. The Colombian Ministers of the Interior, Mines and Energy, and Public Works and Transportation each made statements diminishing the danger pointed out in the report. Privately, Colombian authorities had begun disaster planning. Unfortunately, Nevado del Ruiz erupted before the Colombians had time to put their plans into motion. As predicted, the eruption produced mudflows, ash falls and pyroclastic ash flows.

In just hours after the November 13 eruption, teams of volcanologists from the U.S., Spain, Canada, France, Japan, and Iceland raced to the scene to assist the Colombians in responding to disaster. Detailed studies of the eruption and the changes it brought began. More seismographs and other instruments were brought into the area and installed to gain an even clearer picture of the nature of the mountain.

There is no way to lessen the tragedy of the November 13, 1985 eruption of Nevado del Ruiz, but it did lead to one positive change. A permanent volcano observatory has now been established to monitor the mountain continuously and to serve as a training facility for future Colombian volcanologists and those of other nationalities. The new observatory is the best equipped in all of South America. Scientists and the Colombian government are determined to learn as much about the volcano as they can. Just the day before the November 13 eruption, a team of Colombian geologists had been on the mountain's summit to collect gas samples from fumaroles on the floor of the crater. The geologists had noticed no signs that the volcano was about to erupt. Not enough was known about the mountain, and possibly important warning signs were missed. The new volcano observatory should provide the needed information about the mountain which will lead to ample warning the next time Nevado del Ruiz erupts.

FRIEND AND FOE

They bring death and destruction. They bring life and replenish the soils, oceans, and atmosphere of the earth. Volcanoes can be both our worst nightmares and our best friends. They are a fact of life on earth, and we must coexist with them. Coexisting in safety means studying and monitoring each volcano. We need to understand their nature—what they are made up of, how they are made, why they are where they are, when they have erupted, what they are like when they are quiet, and what they are like when they are active. Each volcano is different, and we need to identify the peculiar warning signs of each in order to predict what they might do next. We need to study each volcano through time to know what it is capable of. We must be prepared to restudy them each time they erupt because the tremendous shattering that takes place during eruptions can change the inside workings of the volcano, causing it to do different things in the future. Only when we know each volcano inside and out, when they are safe and when they are dangerous, can we respond sensibly to them.

GLOSSARY

Aa. A crusty lava composed of jagged, angular blocks.

Active. A volcano that has erupted in historic time.

Ash. Volcanic particles smaller than 0.16 inch (4 mm) in diameter.

Ash flow. An avalanche of heated volcanic ash and gas traveling down the flanks of a volcano. *See also* nuée ardente and pyroclastic flow.

Basalt lava. A blackish, fine-grained lava.

Bombs. Globs of molten lava ejected from a volcano that take on somewhat of a streamlined shape in the air and become hard enough to retain their shape by the time they hit the ground.

Caldera. A large, circular depression usually a mile (1.6 km) or larger in diameter formed by the collapse of a volcano into an empty magma chamber or by the explosion of a cone.

Cinders. Small, bubble-filled grains ejected from a volcano ranging in size from 0.16 inch to 1.25 inches (4 mm to 32 mm).

Cinder cone. A steep-side volcanic cone comprised of cinders.

Columnar basalt. Basalt lava which, during cooling, formed a series of intersecting vertical cracks that give the lava the appearance of columns.

Composite volcano. A steep-sided volcanic cone formed of alternating layers of ash and lava. *See also* Strato-volcano.

Dormant. A volcano that is not currently erupting but is expected to erupt again.

Extensiometer. Instrument for measuring changes in the distance between two points.

Extinct. A volcano that is not expected to erupt again.

Focus. The place within the earth where an earthquake begins.

Fumarole. A vent in the ground from which vapors and fumes rise.

Geothermal power. Mechanical and electrical power derived from the heat of the earth.

Geyser. A more or less regular gusher of hot water emanating from the ground.

Gravity meter. A sensitive device that can detect small changes in gravitational pull.

Hawaiian-type eruption. A relatively quiet volcanic eruption having lava flows, cinder and ash ejection, lava lakes, and lava fountains.

Hot springs. Springs of hot water heated by magma beneath the surface.

Infrared scanner. A device that scans for invisible infrared radiation given off by the heat contained in an object.

Lava. Molten rock on the surface of the earth. Also refers to the rock formed from lava.

Lava dome. A dome-shaped crusty plug of lava built atop the vent of a volcano. With continued pressure from underneath, the dome expands in all directions.

Lava flood. A broad flow of lava issuing from long cracks spanning large basins and plateaus.

Lava tube. A tunnel of hardened lava formed around flowing lava. The flowing lava may completely flow out of the tube at a later time, leaving a cavelike structure.

Lithosphere. The solid portion of the earth.

Magma. Molten rock beneath the surface of the earth.

Nuée ardente eruption. See Ash flow and Peléan eruption.

Pahoehoe. A fluid lava that hardens with a ropy or billowy surface.

Peléan eruption. A powerful eruption of gas-rich magma that produces a dense, pyroclastic blast that may travel vertically or horizontally. If the blast is horizontal, it becomes a high-speed avalanche that obliterates anything in its way.

Plinian eruption. An eruption of gas-rich magma that explodes deep within the volcano, and the volcano's vent acts like a gun barrel as an ash column shoots skyward up to supersonic speeds.

Plug. Hardened lava inside the volcano's vent.

Phreatic eruption. An explosive episode in a volcano in which water has seeped through cracks in the cone and become heated into steam. The steam blows out the plug blocking the vent and cracks more of the cone, permitting more water to seep down to become steam. *See also* Steam eruption.

Pumice. A grayish, glassy rock filled with gas bubble cavities and usually light enough to float on water.

Pyroclastic. Volcanic material (ash, cinders, bombs, etc.) that has been explosively ejected from the volcano's vent.

Pyroclastic flow. A hot cloud of volcanic ash and cinders that rolls down a mountain to envelope and destroy nearly everything in its path. *See also* Ash flow and Peléan eruption.

Pyrometer. An optical device for measuring high temperatures at a distance.

Rift. A deep fissure in the earth's crust.

Satellite cone. A secondary cone forming on the flanks of a larger cone from lava erupting out of a fissure in the larger cone.

Seismic sea wave. An ocean wave caused by earthquakes.

Seismograph. A device for recording earthquake vibrations of the earth measured by a seismometer.

Seismometer. A device for measuring earthquake vibrations in the earth.

Shield volcano. A broad, gently sloping cone formed from repeated eruptions of fluid lava.

Silica. Molecules of silicon and oxygen.

Steam eruption. *See* Phreatic eruption

Strato volcano. *See* Composite volcano.

Strombolian-type eruption. A continuous eruption lasting for many years in which bubbling lava in the cone blasts out globs of lava that collect on the volcano's sides and runs in small lava flows.

Subduction zone. A contact zone between two tectonic plates in which one is thrust beneath the other.

Submarine eruption. Molten lava erupting beneath the surface of the ocean.

Tectonic plates. Large continent-sized rafts of the earth's crust that move.

Theory of plate tectonics. A theory which states the earth's crust is divided up into giant, continent-sized plates that slowly move in relation to each other, causing mountains and rifts along their boundaries.

Thermal plume. A local hot spot rising up from the earth's interior that may be caused by heat from radioactive element decay.

Thermocouple. A pair of wires made of different metals that produce an electric current when in contact with heat. Thermocouples can be used to directly measure temperatures of very hot objects.

Tiltmeter. A device for measuring the tilt of land surfaces.

Tuff. Volcanic rock formed of volcanic fragments smaller than 0.16 inch (4 mm).

Vent. The pathway in a volcano through which magma travels to the surface. Also applies to the opening of geysers and fumaroles.

Volcanic neck. A plug of hardened lava that remains from an extinct volcano when the cone has been worn away.

Volcanologist. A geologist who specializes in the study of volcanoes.

FOR FURTHER READING

Ballard, Robert D. *Exploring Our Living Planet.* Washington, D.C.: National Geographic Society, 1983.

Bullard, Fred M., *Volcanoes of the Earth*, 2nd ed. Austin: University of Texas Press, 1984.

Decker, Robert and Barbara. *Volcano Watching.* Honolulu, Hawaii: Tongg Publishing Co. Ltd., 1984.

Editors of Time-Life Books. *Planet Earth—Volcano.* Alexandria, Va.: Time-Life Books, 1982.

Gray, William R. *Powers of Nature*, Washington, D.C.: National Georgraphic Society, 1978.

Tilling, Robert I. *Volcanoes.* U.S. Geological Survey, 1982.

INDEX